Flip the Flaps
Animal Homes

Judy Allen and Simon Mendez

KINGFISHER

NEW YORK

KINGFISHER
LONDON & NEW YORK

Consultant: David Burnie

Distributed in the U.S. by Macmillan, 175 Fifth Ave., New York, NY 10010
Distributed in Canada by H.B. Fenn and Company Ltd., 34 Nixon Road, Bolton, Ontario L7E 1W2

Library of Congress Cataloging-in-Publication Data has been applied for.

ISBN 978-0-7534-6258-4

Kingfisher books are available for special promotions and premiums. For details contact:
Special Markets Department, Macmillan, 175 Fifth Avenue, New York, NY 10010.

For more information, please visit www.kingfisherpublications.com

First American Edition September 2009
Printed in China
1 3 5 7 9 8 6 4 2
1TR/0309/LFG/UNTD/157MA/C

Contents

Trees

A tree is a little bit like an apartment building, with homes on every level. Birds and squirrels nest in the branches. Small animals live in cracks in the bark. Woodpeckers may live in a hole in the trunk.

squirrel

4   thrush nest

woodpecker

1. What is a squirrel's nest like?

2. Why do woodpeckers peck wood?

3. Which small animals live in trees?

woodpecker
pecking

1. Squirrels build nests, called drays, out of twigs and leaves. Or they may find an empty bird's nest and add a roof.

2. Woodpeckers use their sharp beaks to dig out tasty insects and to make holes for nests.

3. Insects and spiders live on tree bark, and moths rest there, safely hidden.

What lives on tree bark?

peppered moth

bark beetle

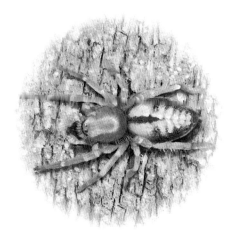

spider

5

Stones

Big stones are home to
small animals that like to
live where it is dark and
damp. Lift one and you
might find earwigs and
pill bugs, springtails
and centipedes.

thrush

snail

1. Do the small animals ever come out from under the stones?

2. Why isn't there a spider in that web?

3. Do worms live under stones?

ladybug

spider rushing out after
feeling the web move

pill bugs

1. Yes. The animals come out to eat. Most eat leaves and soggy wood.

2. The spider hides with one foot on the web. A trapped insect will move the web, and the spider will pounce.

3. Worms live in the soil. But if a stone is on top of soil, there might be worms underneath.

earwig

centipede

ladybug flying

Other animals under stones

worm

millipede

springtail

7

Burrows

A fox's home is called a den. It is a burrow where the female fox has her cubs. She does not make a nest, so the cubs all sleep on the bare ground. Adult foxes mostly sleep outside.

fox cubs playing

8

1. Do all foxes live
   in burrows?

2. Are foxes good at
   digging burrows?

3. Do other animals
   live in burrows?

1. No. Sometimes the den may be under a shed or dug under tree roots.

2. Yes. The female, known as a vixen, digs the den. Or she may just enlarge an old abandoned burrow.

3. Yes, several—badgers, prairie dogs, kingfishers, bumblebees, and mice all live in burrows.

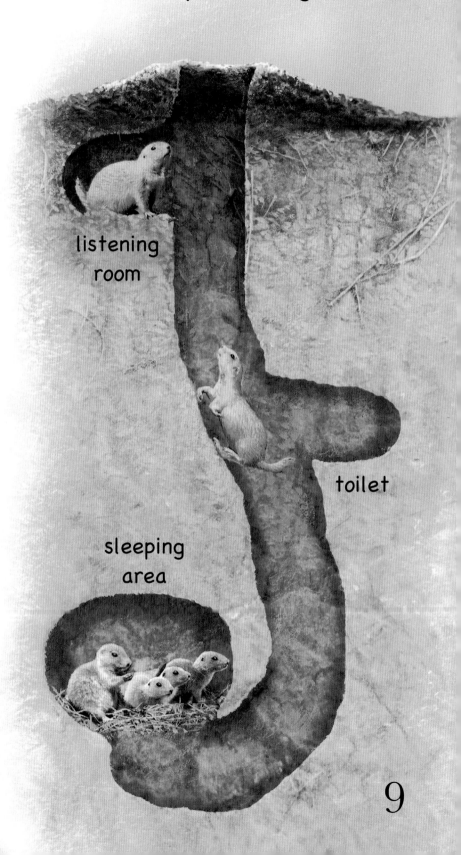

Inside a prairie-dog burrow

listening room

toilet

sleeping area

9

Ponds

Ponds are like tiny worlds.
Dragonflies hover above
while their young live below.
Water boatmen and pond
skaters live on the surface.
Beetles dive. Tadpoles
hatch and turn into frogs.

dragonfly

frog spawn
(eggs)

diving
beetle

water snail

tadpoles

10

1. Do frogs spend all their lives in ponds?

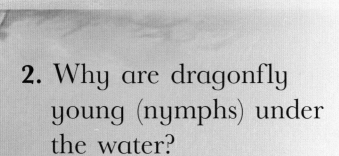

2. Why are dragonfly young (nymphs) under the water?

3. Can pond animals live underwater all the time?

froglet

frog

1. No. Tadpoles hatch from eggs, become froglets, and climb out. Adult frogs live on land and in ponds.

2. Dragonflies lay their eggs on pond plants underwater. The nymphs hatch and live in the pond for two years.

3. Some can. Others, like the diving beetle, take an air bubble down with them.

dragonfly nymph

A dragonfly nymph changes

A dragonfly!

crawling out of old skin

nymph crawling out of pond

11

Shells

Animals with shells already have homes. Some can go inside their shells and sleep safely. Only the hermit crab doesn't grow its own shell. It finds an empty one to move in to.

hermit crab

Lobsters and mussels also have shells.

1. Why are the shells empty?

2. Where do hermit crabs find the empty shells?

3. Do turtles change their shells when they need bigger ones?

turtle

1. When an animal with a shell dies, its body shrivels up and an empty shell is left.

2. A hermit crab finds empty shells on the sea floor. As the crab grows, it has to find a larger shell.

3. No. As with snails, their shells are part of their bodies and grow bigger with them.

hermit crab moving in to a new shell

A snail's shell grows with it

Young snails have small, soft shells.

The shell grows bigger and harder.

Caves

There are sea caves, ice caves,
and land caves where bats
may live. Some bats sleep
in cracks, and others
sleep upside down.

bat

14

1. When do bats sleep?

2. Is it cold in a cave?

3. What else lives
in a bat cave?

bats getting
ready to sleep

1. Bats sleep by day. At night, they fly out to feed.

2. Yes, it may be cold in a cave, but it is sheltered from winter wind and rain.

3. Lots of insects—and spiders and scorpions, too. They are often white if they always live in the dark.

Other animals in a bat cave

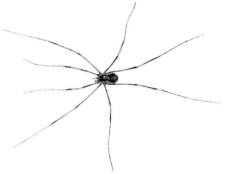

daddy longlegs

cockroach

cave cricket

cave beetle

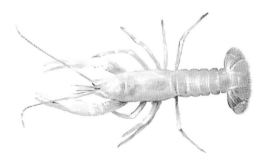

cave crayfish

15

Homebuilders

Beavers use branches and stones to build a lodge in a river or lake. They can bite right through trees with their sharp teeth and chew the wood into useful lengths.

beaver lodge

16

1. Where is the entrance to the beaver lodge?

2. Do beavers eat fish?

3. Do other animals build homes?

1. The lodge entrance is underwater.

2. No. Beavers eat plants, twigs, and tree bark. They store food in the water around the lodge or in a room inside it.

3. Yes. Birds, squirrels, and bees all build homes. The tailorbird makes a home by sewing leaves together.

A tailorbird builds a nest

sewing together leaf edges

safe in the nest

17

Index